# AYESHA

## FROM INNOCENCE TO RESILIENCE

ER. HAIDER KHAN

Made with ❤ on the Notion Press Platform
www.notionpress.com

To my father **Bashir Ahmad Khan**,

Whose unwavering support and encouragement

Have been the guiding light of my life.

To my siblings ,

Who have always been my confidantes

And helped me to pen down my thoughts.

And to my dear friends,

Who have always believed in me and trusted me,

And given me the best suggestions to improve.

# Contents

# Foreword

Life can present us with challenges that are often unexpected, and we may find ourselves struggling to overcome them. In "**Ayesha's Journey: From Innocence to Resilience**," **Er Haider Khan** tells the inspiring story of a woman who faced numerous challenges but never lost hope. Through Ayesha's story, we are reminded of the power of resilience and the human spirit.

As we read this book, we are taken on a journey that reflects the struggles and hardships of many individuals who face adversity. Ayesha's story is a testament to the fact that, no matter how difficult our circumstances may seem, we can find the courage and determination to overcome them. Her story is a beacon of hope for all those who have experienced loss, grief, betrayal, or abuse.

Er Haider Khan, with his exceptional storytelling, brings to life the story of Ayesha and the struggles of people in the Kashmir region. His work as an author and advocate highlights important issues and serves as an inspiration for others to stand up and fight for justice.

# Preface

When I first met Ayesha, she had already begun to rebuild her life. Despite the traumas and hardships she had faced, she radiated a sense of strength and resilience that I found inspiring. As I listened to her story, I knew that it was one that needed to be told.

The purpose of this book is to share Ayesha's journey from innocence to resilience with the world. Her story is one that will resonate with many, and I hope that it will serve as a source of inspiration and hope for those who may be struggling.

In writing this book, I have attempted to remain as faithful to Ayesha's story as possible. While some details have been changed to protect her identity and privacy, the essence of her story remains unchanged.

This book is also an attempt to highlight the issues that Ayesha and countless others like her face. The struggle for women's rights and the fight against abuse and discrimination are ongoing battles, and it is my hope that this book will serve as a call to action for readers.

# Acknowledgements

- Er. Haider Khan

I Myself Mohammad Shafi Khan known by my pen name Er.haider khan would also like to thank my family Mostly **Tr. BAshir Ahmad Khan** my father and friends for their unwavering support throughout the writing process. Your encouragement and belief in me have been invaluable.

I owe a debt of gratitude to the many individuals and organizations who work tirelessly to support women's rights and combat abuse and discrimination. Your work is a constant reminder of the power of the human spirit to overcome even the greatest of challenges.

I would like to express my appreciation to my editor, whose guidance and feedback helped to shape this book into its final form. Your expertise and support have been invaluable.

Finally, I would like to thank the readers of this book. It is my hope that Ayesha's story will resonate with you and serve as a source of inspiration and hope.

# Prologue

> "*Ayesha had always been a fighter. Even as a young girl, she had a fierce determination that belied her age. Growing up in the idyllic countryside of Kashmir, she had a carefree childhood filled with laughter and adventure. But tragedy struck when her father passed away, leaving her family reeling with grief.*"

It was in the aftermath of this loss that Ayesha's resilience truly began to shine. She struggled to come to terms with her father's death, but with the support of her mother and siblings, she began to rebuild her life.

But the challenges that lay ahead were far greater than anything Ayesha had ever imagined. As she grew older, she encountered betrayal, violence, and heartbreak. And yet, through it all, she never lost her sense of hope.

This book is Ayesha's story. It is a story of loss and pain, but also of strength and resilience. It is a testament to the human spirit and the power of hope. And above all, it is a call to action, a reminder that we must all do our part to fight for women's rights and combat abuse and discrimination.

As you read Ayesha's story, I hope that you will be inspired by her courage and resilience. I hope that you will be moved to take action and make a difference in the lives of those who face similar challenges. And I hope that you will come away with a greater appreciation for the power of the human spirit to overcome even the greatest of hardships.

# Ayesha's Escape And New Beginning

Ayesha had hit rock bottom. She was trapped in a loveless and abusive marriage, and she had lost all hope for a happy future. She had tried everything she could think of to make things better, but nothing worked. Her husband was cruel and manipulative, and he seemed to take pleasure in making her feel small and insignificant.

One day, Ayesha decided she had had enough. She packed a bag and left the house, not looking back. She didn't know where she was going, but she knew she couldn't stay with her husband any longer. She wandered the streets aimlessly, trying to figure out what to do next.

As she walked, she saw a man sitting on a bench, reading a book. He looked up as she approached, and their eyes met. Ayesha felt like she could trust him, even though she didn't know him. She told him her story, and he listened with compassion and understanding.

The man, whose name was Ali, was kind and gentle. He offered to help Ayesha in any way he could, and she was grateful for his support. He took her to a shelter for women, where she could stay until she figured out her next steps.

At the shelter, Ayesha met other women who had been through similar experiences. She felt a sense of community and support that she had never felt before. She started to open up to the other women, sharing her story and listening to theirs.

Over time, Ayesha started to heal. She went to therapy and learned how to cope with her trauma. She also started to think about what she wanted for her future. She had always wanted to go to college, but her husband had discouraged her. Now, with the support of the women at the shelter, she decided to enroll in classes.

Ayesha threw herself into her studies. She worked hard and earned good grades, and she felt proud of herself for the first time in a long time. She also started volunteering at the shelter, helping other women who were going through similar experiences.

One day, Ali came to the shelter to visit Ayesha. They had grown close over the past few months, and Ayesha had started to develop feelings for him. He was kind, caring, and understanding, and she felt safe with him.

As they talked, Ali confessed that he had feelings for Ayesha too. She was surprised but happy. They started dating, taking things slow and enjoying each other's company.

Ayesha was hesitant to get into another relationship so soon after leaving her husband, but Ali was different. He treated her with respect and kindness, and he never made her feel small or insignificant. Ayesha fell in love with him, and he became her rock.

After a year of dating, Ali proposed to Ayesha. She said yes, and they got married in a small ceremony at the shelter. Ayesha felt like she had finally found the happiness and security she had been searching for.

Ayesha graduated from college with honors, and she started working as a counselor at the shelter. She helped other women who were going through what she had gone through, and she felt fulfilled knowing that she was making a difference in their lives.

Ayesha's life had taken a turn for the better. She had gone through a lot of pain and suffering, but she had come out the other side stronger and more resilient. She had learned that there are good people in the world who will help you when you need it most, and that it's important to be cautious and to trust your instincts when it comes to others. Her story is a testament to the power of resilience, courage, and the human spirit.

# ONE

# A Carefree Childhood

Ayesha had a relatively carefree childhood in a small town. Her parents were loving and doting, and she was the apple of their eye. They did their best to provide her with everything she needed, even though they didn't have much. They never let their financial struggles dampen their love and affection for Ayesha.

As a child, Ayesha had no grand dreams or aspirations. She was happy just being a child, playing with her friends, and spending time with her family. She loved to read books, especially fairy tales, and she would lose herself in their magical worlds for hours on end. Her favorite fairy tale was Cinderella, and she would imagine herself as the beautiful princess, waiting for her prince to come and rescue her from her mundane life.

Ayesha didn't have much exposure to the world outside her small town, but she was content with her simple life. She would often go for long walks in the fields, admiring the beauty of nature and daydreaming about the future. She didn't have a clear idea of what she wanted to do with her life, but she longed to earn respect and find happiness.

One of her fondest childhood memories was of a day when her father took her to a nearby city. She had never been to a city before, and everything seemed so exciting and new to her. They visited a mall, and Ayesha was mesmerized by the glittering lights, the fancy clothes, and the exotic foods. She begged her father to buy her a new dress, and he didn't disappoint her. Ayesha felt like a princess in her new dress, and she treasured it like a precious possession.

But Ayesha's life took a drastic turn when her father died in a car accident. Ayesha was devastated, and her world turned dark. She couldn't comprehend the fact that her father was gone forever. She struggled with her emotions and tried to move forward, but it wasn't easy. She felt alone and helpless, and she didn't have anyone to turn to. Her mother was also struggling with her grief and couldn't provide the emotional support that Ayesha needed.

Ayesha's childhood innocence was shattered, and she was forced to grow up faster than she wanted to. She had to learn to be strong and resilient, even though she felt like crumbling. She took on more responsibilities at home, helping her mother with the household chores and taking care of her younger siblings. She tried her best to cope with her father's loss, but it wasn't enough.

As Ayesha grew older, she faced more challenges. She had to deal with the expectations of society, which demanded that she conform to certain norms and values. She was also struggling with her own identity, trying to figure out who she was and what she wanted from life. She had no one to turn to for guidance, and she often felt lost and confused.

Despite the challenges she faced, Ayesha never lost her sense of optimism and hope. She believed that there was something better waiting for her in the future, and she refused to give up on her dreams. She worked hard in school, hoping to get a good education and a decent job. She also volunteered at a local orphanage, where she found solace in helping others.

Through it all, Ayesha held on to the memory of her father, who had always encouraged her to be strong and independent. She knew that he was watching over her from above, and that gave her the strength to keep going, even in the darkest of times.

As Ayesha approached adulthood, she knew that her life was

# TWO

# THE TRAGIC LOSS OF AYESHA'S FATHER

Ayesha's world came crashing down when she lost her father in a car accident. She was just sixteen years old, and the loss was devastating. Ayesha's father had been her rock, her mentor, and her biggest supporter. He had always been there for her, and now he was gone.

The days following her father's death were a blur for Ayesha. She felt numb, like she was living in a dream. Her family and friends tried to support her, but she didn't want to talk about what had happened. She was too lost in her grief to communicate with anyone.

As time passed, Ayesha's grief turned into anger. She was angry at the world for taking her father away, and she was angry at herself for not being able to save him. She blamed herself for not being there with him, and she couldn't shake the feeling that she could have prevented his death.

Ayesha's anger manifested in different ways. She lashed out at her family and friends, pushing them away with hurtful words and actions. She stopped caring about school and her future, feeling like there was no point in trying. She began to isolate herself, spending hours alone in her room or wandering the streets of her small town.

Ayesha's mother was also struggling with her grief, and the two of them had a strained relationship. They would argue and fight over the smallest things, and Ayesha felt like her mother didn't understand her pain. She felt alone and abandoned, like she had lost both her father and her mother.

It wasn't until Ayesha met a therapist that she began to open up about her feelings. The therapist helped her understand that her anger was a normal part of the grieving process, and that it was okay to feel the way she did. Ayesha began to talk more about her father, sharing memories and stories about him that made her smile.

As she started to heal, Ayesha also began to think about her future. She realized that her father would have wanted her to succeed, and that she couldn't give up on her dreams. She started to study harder and focus on her education, determined to make her father proud.

Over time, Ayesha's anger began to fade, replaced by a sense of determination and purpose. She started to see a therapist regularly and began to work through her grief. She reconnected with her mother and started to rebuild their relationship. She even began to think about the possibility of finding love and starting a family of her own.

The loss of Ayesha's father was a turning point in her life. It was a tragedy that she would never forget, but it was also a catalyst for change. Ayesha learned that she was stronger than she ever thought possible, and that she had the power to shape her own future.

# THREE

# Ayesha's Struggle with Grief

The days following the funeral were the hardest for Ayesha. She felt like a part of her had died with her father, and she didn't know how to move forward. The house felt empty without him, and every corner reminded her of his absence.

At first, Ayesha tried to keep herself busy. She cleaned the house, cooked meals, and took care of her younger siblings. She wanted to be strong for them, but it was difficult. Her own pain was so deep that it consumed her, and she found herself crying often, sometimes for hours at a time.

Ayesha's mother was also struggling with the loss of her husband, but she was better at hiding it. She spent most of her time in her room, and when she did come out, she put on a brave face. Ayesha admired her mother's strength, but it made her feel even more alone.

As the days turned into weeks, Ayesha's sadness turned into anger. She couldn't understand why her father had been taken from her. He was a good man who had worked hard to provide for his family, and he deserved to live a long and happy life. Ayesha felt like the world was unfair, and she resented anyone who seemed happy.

One day, Ayesha was walking home from the market when she saw a group of children playing in the park. They were laughing and chasing each other, and Ayesha felt a pang of envy. She wondered how they could be so carefree when her world had been turned upside down.

As she walked past the park, she heard a familiar voice. It was her father's best friend, Mr. Khan. Ayesha had always liked Mr. Khan. He was kind and funny, and he had a way of making her feel better even on her worst days.

"Hey Ayesha," he said, waving at her. "How are you doing?"

Ayesha forced a smile. "I'm okay," she lied.

Mr. Khan looked at her sympathetically. "I know it's hard, Ayesha. But your father wouldn't want you to be sad all the time. He was a happy man who loved his family. He wouldn't want to see you suffer."

Ayesha nodded, but she didn't feel any better. She couldn't imagine a life without her father, and the thought of trying to be happy again seemed impossible.

Over the next few weeks, Ayesha tried to distract herself. She watched TV, read books, and spent time with her siblings. But no matter what she did, she couldn't escape her grief. It was always there, like a heavy weight on her chest.

One day, Ayesha was in her room, looking through old photo albums. She found a picture of her and her father at the beach. They were both smiling, and Ayesha remembered how much fun they had that day. She felt a surge of sadness, but then something else - a sense of gratitude.

Her father may be gone, but he had given her so much during his lifetime. He had loved her, taught her, and made her feel special. She realized that she had to be grateful for the time they had together, and that he would always be a part of her.

Slowly, Ayesha's sadness began to lift. She still missed her father, but she started to see the good in life again. She realized that she had a lot to be thankful for, and that her father's memory would always be with her.

As she started to come out of her grief, Ayesha also began to think about her future. She knew that her father would

# FOUR

# Ayesha's First Encounter with Betrayal

Ayesha's life had been shattered by the tragic loss of her father, but as she tried to pick up the pieces, another challenge was lurking around the corner. She was only 18 when she had her first encounter with betrayal, and it would shape the course of her life for years to come.

It was a warm summer evening, and Ayesha was on her way home from the market. She was carrying a basket of groceries and feeling content. She had managed to get everything she needed for her mother and siblings, and she was proud of herself for being so responsible.

As she was walking down the street, she heard someone calling her name. It was a man she knew vaguely from the neighbourhood. He was a few years older than her, and he had always seemed friendly. Ayesha smiled and said hello, expecting a casual conversation.

But as they started talking, Ayesha began to feel uneasy. The man was asking her questions that made her uncomfortable, and his tone was becoming increasingly suggestive. She tried to politely end the conversation and continue walking, but he persisted.

Before she knew it, the man had grabbed her by the arm and pulled her into a dark alley. Ayesha was terrified. She had never experienced anything like this before. She tried to scream, but the man covered her mouth with his hand.

He proceeded to tease and taunt her, making her feel inferior and unworthy. He told her that no one would ever want her, and that she was lucky to have him paying attention to her. Ayesha was confused and scared. She had always been taught to respect her elders and be polite, but this man was violating her boundaries in the most heinous way.

After what seemed like an eternity, the man finally let Ayesha go. He warned her not to tell anyone about what had happened, or else he would hurt her and her family. Ayesha was too afraid to speak out. She felt ashamed and alone.

For weeks, Ayesha was haunted by the memory of that night. She tried to go about her daily routine, but her mind was constantly consumed by fear and anxiety. She didn't know who to turn to or how to seek help. She felt like she was drowning in a sea of despair.

It wasn't until Ayesha had a chance encounter with a kind stranger that she began to find some solace. She was walking down the street one day when a man approached her. He had seen her around before, and he had always been friendly. Ayesha was hesitant at first, but something about the man's demeanour made her feel safe.

The man asked Ayesha if she was okay, and she burst into tears. She told him everything that had happened to her, and he listened with empathy and understanding. He assured her that what had happened was not her fault, and that she deserved to be treated with respect and kindness.

For the first time since that fateful night in the alley, Ayesha felt like someone was on her side. She felt like there was hope. The man offered to help her in any way he could, and Ayesha felt like she had finally found someone she could rely on.

But as she was about to find out, betrayal can come from unexpected places.

# FIVE

# Ayesha's Descent into Darkness

Ayesha's life had taken a turn for the worse. She was alone, helpless, and trapped in a situation she couldn't escape from. Her husband treated her poorly, making her feel small and insignificant. She tried to be patient, hoping that things would get better, but they only got worse.

Ayesha had become a shell of her former self. She had lost all sense of hope and purpose. Every day was a struggle, and she couldn't see a way out of her situation. She was stuck in a never-ending cycle of abuse and torment, and it was slowly breaking her.

Her husband had become increasingly violent, and Ayesha lived in constant fear. She was too afraid to leave, too afraid to fight back. She felt like she had no one to turn to, no one who would listen or understand.

One day, Ayesha was walking down the street when she saw a woman who had bruises on her face. She knew exactly what had happened to her. She had seen it before. She felt sorry for the woman, but she also felt a sense of kinship. She knew what it was like to be in that woman's shoes.

Ayesha decided to reach out to the woman. She offered her a kind word, a sympathetic ear. The woman opened up to her, telling her the horrors of her life. Ayesha listened intently, and it was as if she was hearing her own story being told to her.

Over time, Ayesha and the woman became close friends. They shared their stories and their pain, and they found solace in each other's company. They would meet secretly, and talk for hours on end. They would share their hopes and dreams, and they would encourage each other to keep going.

One day, Ayesha's husband found out about her secret meetings with the woman. He was furious, and he beat her mercilessly. Ayesha was left bruised and battered, but she didn't give up. She knew that she had to keep fighting, for herself and for her friend.

Ayesha started to plan her escape. She knew that it wouldn't be easy, but she also knew that she couldn't stay in her current situation. She reached out to the man who had hit her with his car, the man who had changed her life. He offered to help her in any way he could, and she was grateful for his support.

Together, they planned her escape. Ayesha left her husband in the dead of night, taking only the clothes on her back. She didn't look back, and she didn't regret her decision. She was finally free.

Over time, Ayesha started to rebuild her life. She found a job, a small apartment, and a sense of purpose. She started to feel like herself again, and she started to dream once more. She would often think about her friend, the woman who had shared her pain. She wondered if she had ever been able to escape.

Ayesha's story is a testament to the power of the human spirit. It is a story of resilience, courage, and the will to survive. Despite everything she had been through, Ayesha never gave up. She kept fighting, and she found a way to break free from the darkness that had consumed her.

# SIX

# THE HIT AND RUN

Ayesha woke up in a hospital bed, her head pounding and her body aching. She couldn't remember what had happened, but she knew something was wrong. She tried to move, but the pain in her body was too intense. She looked around and saw a nurse walking towards her.

"Miss Ayesha, you're awake. Thank God. We were worried about you," the nurse said.

"What happened to me?" Ayesha asked, her voice hoarse.

"You were hit by a car. The driver brought you here. You're lucky to be alive," the nurse replied.

Ayesha couldn't believe what she was hearing. She had been hit by a car? She tried to remember what had happened before the accident, but everything was a blur. The nurse gave her some pain medication and told her to rest. Ayesha closed her eyes and drifted off to sleep.

When she woke up, her head was clearer, but her body still hurt. She tried to move, and this time the pain was bearable. She sat up and saw a man sitting in a chair next to her bed. He was holding her hand, and she could see the concern on his face.

"Who are you?" Ayesha asked.

"I'm the man who hit you with my car. I'm so sorry," the man said, his voice filled with regret.

Ayesha looked at him and felt a strange sense of familiarity. She couldn't place him, but she felt like she knew him from somewhere. She didn't know what to say, so she just looked at him in silence.

"I know this might sound strange, but I feel like I know you. Have we met before?" Ayesha asked.

The man smiled, and his eyes filled with warmth. "Yes, we have. We went to school together. My name is Ali."

Ayesha's eyes widened in surprise. She couldn't believe that the man who hit her was someone she knew from school. She had lost touch with most of her classmates over the years, but she remembered Ali. He was always kind and respectful, and he had a gentle nature.

"Ali, what happened?" Ayesha asked.

"I was driving home from work, and I didn't see you until it was too late. I swerved to avoid hitting you, but I couldn't stop in time. I'm so sorry, Ayesha. I never meant to hurt you," Ali said, his voice full of remorse.

Ayesha looked at him and saw the sincerity in his eyes. She knew that he wasn't lying, and she could sense the regret in his voice. She didn't know what to say, so she just sat there in silence.

Over the next few days, Ayesha stayed in the hospital, recovering from her injuries. Ali visited her every day, bringing her flowers and books to read. They talked about their school days and caught up on old times. Ayesha found herself enjoying his company, and she looked forward to his visits.

One day, as they were talking, Ali asked Ayesha if she would like to go out with him. Ayesha was hesitant at first, but she eventually agreed. They went to a restaurant and had dinner, talking and laughing like old friends. Ayesha felt like she had known Ali all her life, and she felt safe and secure in his company.

As the weeks went by, Ayesha and Ali grew closer. He helped her through the difficult time after her father's death, and he listened to her when she needed someone to talk to. Ayesha felt like she had finally found someone who understood her, someone she could trust.

One day,

# SEVEN

# A Chance Encounter with Kindness

Ayesha's heart was heavy as she lay in the hospital bed. The accident had left her battered and bruised, but she was grateful to be alive. As she lay there, she couldn't help but wonder why life had been so cruel to her. She had lost her father, and now she was alone, with no one to turn to.

As she lay in the hospital, she began to sink into a deep depression. She couldn't imagine going back to her old life, where she was abused and mistreated. She felt like she had nothing to live for, and she couldn't find a reason to get out of bed.

It was during this dark time that Ayesha had a chance encounter with kindness. One day, as she was taking a walk around the hospital grounds, she saw a man sitting on a bench. He looked up as she approached, and she was struck by his kind eyes and gentle smile.

"Hello," he said. "Are you okay?"

Ayesha hesitated for a moment before answering. She didn't know this man, and she wasn't used to people showing her kindness.

"I'm fine," she said, trying to sound convincing.

The man looked at her with concern. "Are you sure?" he asked.

Ayesha sighed. "No, I'm not okay," she admitted. "My life is a mess, and I don't know what to do."

The man listened patiently as Ayesha poured out her heart. She told him about her father's death, her abusive husband, and the accident that had brought her to the hospital. She talked about her despair and her fear that she would never find happiness.

The man listened with compassion, and when Ayesha was finished, he put a hand on her shoulder. "I'm sorry for everything you've been through," he said. "But you're not alone. There are people who care about you and want to help you."

Ayesha didn't know what to say. She had never met anyone like this man before, someone who seemed to genuinely care about her.

"Who are you?" she asked.

The man smiled. "My name is Ali," he said. "And I'm just a guy who wants to help you. Will you let me?"

Ayesha nodded, tears streaming down her face. She felt like she had nothing to lose.

Over the next few days, Ali visited Ayesha in the hospital every day. He brought her food, books to read, and most importantly, he brought her hope. He told her stories of people who had overcome incredible obstacles, and he encouraged her to believe in herself.

Slowly but surely, Ayesha began to feel better. She felt like she had a purpose in life, and she began to look forward to the future. Ali had given her something that no one else had ever given her before – the gift of hope.

When Ayesha was finally released from the hospital, Ali helped her find a place to stay. He made sure she had everything she needed to start a new life. Ayesha was grateful for his kindness, and she knew that she could never repay him for all that he had done for her.

But that didn't stop her from trying.

Over the next few months, Ayesha worked hard to get back on her feet. She found a job and started saving money. She also started to see Ali in a new light. She had always appreciated his kindness, but now she was beginning to see him as more than just a friend.

It wasn't long before Ayesha realized that she was in love with Ali. He had been there for her when she needed him most, and she couldn

# EIGHT

# AYESHA'S MARRIAGE TO A MONSTER

Ayesha's life had never been easy, but she thought she had finally found a way out of the darkness. She had married the man who had saved her from her abusive ex-husband, and she believed that her troubles were finally over. But she was wrong.

Ayesha's new husband, Farhan, had a charming facade, but underneath he was a monster. He was controlling, manipulative, and abusive, both physically and emotionally. He made her feel like she was worthless and that she had no other options.

At first, Ayesha tried to convince herself that things would get better, that Farhan was just going through a difficult time. She thought that if she could be patient and understanding, he would change. But the abuse only got worse. Farhan was never satisfied, and he seemed to take pleasure in hurting Ayesha.

Ayesha tried to leave him several times, but Farhan always found her and dragged her back. He made her feel like she had no other options, no way out. Ayesha felt trapped and alone, and she began to lose hope.

The abuse started to take a toll on Ayesha's physical and mental health. She lost weight, stopped eating, and became withdrawn. She was always afraid of Farhan's next attack and never knew when it would happen.

One day, Ayesha decided that she couldn't take it anymore. She made a plan to escape from Farhan's grasp and start a new life. She packed a bag and left in the middle of the night. She had nowhere to go, no money, and no friends or family to turn to. But she knew that she couldn't stay with Farhan any longer.

Ayesha spent the next few weeks on the streets, begging for food and shelter. She was weak, sick, and barely holding on. But she refused to give up. She knew that she had to keep fighting, that she deserved a better life than the one Farhan had given her.

One day, Ayesha met a woman named Reena, who took her in and helped her get back on her feet. Reena was a survivor herself, having escaped an abusive relationship many years ago. She understood what Ayesha had gone through and offered her a place to stay and a job at her bakery.

Ayesha was grateful for Reena's help and support. She started working at the bakery and slowly began to rebuild her life. She made new friends and started to feel like she belonged somewhere. She even met a man named Zain, who treated her with kindness and respect.

Ayesha and Zain fell in love, and he asked her to marry him. Ayesha was hesitant at first, afraid that history would repeat itself. But Zain was different from Farhan. He was gentle, kind, and loving, and he never raised his voice or his hand to her.

Ayesha said yes, and they were married in a small ceremony. Ayesha felt happy for the first time in a long time. She had found someone who loved her for who she was, who saw her worth, and who supported her dreams.

Ayesha's story is one of strength, resilience, and the power of love. She never gave up, even when the odds were against her. She found a way out of the darkness and into the light, and she learned that happiness is possible, even after so much pain and suffering.

# NINE

# Ayesha's Escape and New Beginning

Ayesha had hit rock bottom. She was trapped in a loveless and abusive marriage, and she had lost all hope for a happy future. She had tried everything she could think of to make things better, but nothing worked. Her husband was cruel and manipulative, and he seemed to take pleasure in making her feel small and insignificant.

One day, Ayesha decided she had had enough. She packed a bag and left the house, not looking back. She didn't know where she was going, but she knew she couldn't stay with her husband any longer. She wandered the streets aimlessly, trying to figure out what to do next.

As she walked, she saw a man sitting on a bench, reading a book. He looked up as she approached, and their eyes met. Ayesha felt like she could trust him, even though she didn't know him. She told him her story, and he listened with compassion and understanding.

The man, whose name was Ali, was kind and gentle. He offered to help Ayesha in any way he could, and she was grateful for his support. He took her to a shelter for women, where she could stay until she figured out her next steps.

At the shelter, Ayesha met other women who had been through similar experiences. She felt a sense of community and support that she had never felt before. She started to open up to the other women, sharing her story and listening to theirs.

Over time, Ayesha started to heal. She went to therapy and learned how to cope with her trauma. She also started to think about what she wanted for her future. She had always wanted to go to college, but her husband had discouraged her. Now, with the support of the women at the shelter, she decided to enroll in classes.

Ayesha threw herself into her studies. She worked hard and earned good grades, and she felt proud of herself for the first time in a long time. She also started volunteering at the shelter, helping other women who were going through similar experiences.

One day, Ali came to the shelter to visit Ayesha. They had grown close over the past few months, and Ayesha had started to develop feelings for him. He was kind, caring, and understanding, and she felt safe with him.

As they talked, Ali confessed that he had feelings for Ayesha too. She was surprised but happy. They started dating, taking things slow and enjoying each other's company.

Ayesha was hesitant to get into another relationship so soon after leaving her husband, but Ali was different. He treated her with respect and kindness, and he never made her feel small or insignificant. Ayesha fell in love with him, and he became her rock.

After a year of dating, Ali proposed to Ayesha. She said yes, and they got married in a small ceremony at the shelter. Ayesha felt like she had finally found the happiness and security she had been searching for.

Ayesha graduated from college with honors, and she started working as a counselor at the shelter. She helped other women who were going through what she had gone through, and she felt fulfilled knowing that she was making a difference in their lives.

Ayesha's life had taken a turn for the better. She had gone through a lot of pain and suffering, but she had come out the other side stronger and more resilient. She had learned that there are good people in the world who will help you when you need it most, and that it's important to be cautious and to trust your instincts when it comes to others. Her story is a testament to the power of resilience, courage, and the human spirit.

# TEN

# Ayesha Finds Love and Happiness

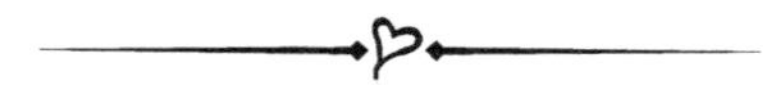

Ayesha was grateful for the kindness and support of her new friend, Ali. He had been there for her when she had nowhere else to turn, and she had grown to rely on him for comfort and strength. As they spent more time together, Ayesha realized that she was beginning to develop feelings for Ali. She tried to suppress them, knowing that it was too soon after her traumatic experience with her ex-husband, but she couldn't help how she felt.

Ali, too, had grown fond of Ayesha. He admired her resilience and her determination to move forward in spite of the challenges she had faced. He felt protective of her, and he wanted to do everything he could to help her rebuild her life. As they spent more time together, he began to see her in a new light - not just as a friend, but as a potential partner.

One day, Ali mustered up the courage to tell Ayesha how he felt. He took her to a beautiful park near their home and sat with her on a bench overlooking a pond. He told her that he cared for her deeply and that he wanted to be more than just friends. Ayesha was taken aback, but she didn't feel afraid or uncomfortable. She had grown to trust Ali, and she knew that he would never hurt her.

Ayesha confessed that she had feelings for Ali, too, but that she was scared to pursue a new relationship. She had been through so much, and she didn't want to risk getting hurt again. Ali reassured her that he would never hurt her and that he would always be there for her, no matter what. He told her that he loved her and that he wanted to make her happy.

Over time, Ayesha and Ali grew closer. They spent long days together, exploring the city and discovering new places. They laughed together and talked for hours about everything and anything. They supported each other through the ups and downs of life, and they always had each other's backs.

Eventually, Ali proposed to Ayesha. He took her to a beautiful restaurant in the heart of the city and got down on one knee. He told her that he wanted to spend the rest of his life with her, and he asked her to marry him. Ayesha was overwhelmed with emotion. She had never expected to find someone like Ali, someone who loved her for who she was and accepted her past without judgment. She said yes, and they hugged each other tightly, knowing that their lives were about to change forever.

Ayesha and Ali's wedding was a joyous occasion. They invited all of their friends and family, and they exchanged vows in a beautiful outdoor ceremony. Ayesha wore a white dress, and Ali wore a black suit. They looked like the perfect couple, and everyone could see the love in their eyes.

After the wedding, Ayesha and Ali moved into a small apartment together. They started a new life, filled with love, happiness, and hope. Ayesha pursued her dream of becoming a teacher, and Ali worked as a freelance writer. They had their struggles, of course - every couple does - but they always managed to work through their issues with patience and understanding.

Years passed, and Ayesha and Ali's love only grew stronger. They had children, and they watched them grow into bright, happy, and confident young adults. They traveled the world together, exploring new cultures and making memories that would last a lifetime. They never forgot the challenges they had faced in the past, but they didn't dwell on them, either. They focused on the present, and they relished every moment they had together.

In the end, Ayesha realized

# ELEVEN

# The Power of Resilience and the Human Spirit

Ayesha had been through so much in her life, but she refused to give up. She had been betrayed, abused, and broken, but she had managed to overcome it all. Her experiences had taught her that the human spirit is incredibly resilient and can endure even the most difficult of circumstances.

She had learned to be cautious and to trust her instincts when it came to people. She had learned to be strong and to fight for what she believed in. She had learned that there are good people in the world who will help you when you need it most.

Ayesha had also learned the importance of self-care and self-love. She knew that she needed to take care of herself in order to be able to help others. She had learned to value herself and to never let anyone make her feel small or unworthy.

Over time, Ayesha had built a new life for herself. She had a supportive and loving husband, a stable job, and a strong network of friends and family. She was finally able to live the life she had always wanted.

Through her experiences, Ayesha had also become an advocate for women's rights and for those who have experienced abuse. She shared her story with others in the hopes of inspiring them to never give up, no matter how difficult their circumstances may be.

Ayesha had learned that the power of resilience and the human spirit is truly remarkable. She had been able to overcome the most difficult of circumstances and build a new life for herself. Her story is a testament to the strength of the human spirit and the power of hope.

# Thank You

**Bye And Share Love And Happyness**

**Er Haider Khan**

Lots of love

Printed by Libri Plureos GmbH in Hamburg,
Germany